S0-DFJ-965

Companion

WORKBOOK

to the

5 Love

LANGUAGES

Do The Relationship Work

This publication is part of a series of products and publications. For more information, please visit: http://www.JournalsPlannersAndMore.com/.

Copyright 2019 Julie Ann Price, Beauty With A Cause, LLC.

ALL RIGHTS RESERVED.

One or more global copyright treaties protect the information in this document. This journal is not intended to provide exact details or advice. This book is for informational purposes only. Author reserves the right to make any changes necessary to maintain the integrity of the information held within. This journal is not presented as legal or accounting advice. All rights reserved, including the right of reproduction in whole or in part in any form. No parts of this book may be reproduced in any form without written permission of the copyright owner.

NOTICE OF LIABILITY

In no event shall the author or the publisher be responsible or liable for any loss of profits or other commercial or personal damages, including but not limited to special incidental, consequential, or any other damages, in connection with or arising out of furnishing, performance or use of this book.

This workbook is intended to help you strengthen your romantic relationship using the 5 love languages described in the original book.

It is meant to supplement the book, not act as a replacement for reading the book itself.

This book is in no way affiliated with the original book, The 5 Love Languages, by Gary Chapman.

You can purchase the original book on Amazon.

To access the PDF version of this workbook, go to the last page.

The above link is an affiliate link which means, at no additional cost to you, I may make a small commission.

I hope you find value
in this workbook

Be sure to check out my other
workbooks, planners & journals
at
JournalsPlannerAndMore.com.

I APPRECIATE YOUR REVIEWS!

I am a small independent author. Your reviews on Amazon
are very important to me. Reviews help others decide if
they want to purchase this book.

If you can spare a few minutes, please log into your
Amazon account, click on your past purchases and leave a
review for this book. I would appreciate it immensely.

SPECIALS

I regularly offer specials to my readers who join my VIP
Club. Each month they get news about the latest releases
and a heads up when a book will be free on Amazon. They
also benefit from members-only specials, advance copies
and contests.

If you want to get the insider information - join the club at
JournalsPlannersAndMore.com

"Love is a choice you make everyday."

Gary Chapman

The 5 Love Languages

The object of love is not getting something you want but doing something for the well-being of the one you love.

Gary Chapman

Overview

You've read the bestselling book, The 5 Love Languages, by Gary Chapman. Now, it's time to put what you have discovered into action.

This workbook will help you strengthen your relationship through actively planning to speak your partner's love language and asking for what you need according to your own language.

You will start by brainstorming all the things that you could do for your partner and all the things you would like your partner to do for you.

Then you will create a plan for actually doing those things each month. You will reflect on the response and feedback you get from your efforts so that you can refine your approach.

Remember each language has many different dialects and what you try first may not be on target. Don't give up. Keep trying to speak the same language but in a different way.

For example, spending quality time could mean doing a project together or it could mean enjoying the planning but not the actual doing of a project together.

It could mean going out to dinner together or it could mean making a meal together. Only through experimentation will you figure out what fills your partner's love tank.

It is assumed that you have already determined your and your partner's top two love languages from the original book text, specifically the quiz on the back pages.

The purpose of this workbook is to help you:
- Refine which of the love languages is really the strongest for you and your partner
- Discover the specific dialect of your partner's language
- Experiment with different actions that fill your partner's love tank
- Get you into the practice of asking for what you need to fill your own tank
- Build a habit of filling one another's tanks every week

Only through ongoing action, repetition, and awareness, can you regularly speak the love language of your partner and have a long-lasting, beautiful relationship.

Let's get to work.

The 5 Languages

What are your and your partner's top two love languages?

The 5 Languages are:
- Affirmations or Words of Love
- Quality Time
- Receiving Gifts
- Acts of Service
- Physical Touch

My top two love languages are:

_____

_____

My partner's top two love languages are:

_____

_____

If your partner hasn't taken the quiz to determine his/her love language, pick the two you think are most likely. Through experimentation you will be able to uncover the most accurate languages.

On the next 2 pages, brainstorm some of the things you can do for your partner and that you would like your partner to do for you.

If your partner is on board, have him/her complete a set of pages too.

Objectives

Before we dive in, let's spend a few minutes identifying why you want to improve your relationship and what you would like to be the outcome of the work you are about to do.

If you don't have a purpose or a mission, it will be hard for you to commit to doing the work. Answer the questions below and if your partner is on board, have him/her complete the same set of questions on this and the next page too..

Compare your answers to see where you are in agreement and to learn what one another's perspectives are. By having a shared understanding of why you are doing this, you increase your chances of success tremendously.

Why do you want to improve your relationship?

_____

_____

_____

_____

_____

What do you believe is possible for your relationship?

_____

_____

_____

_____

_____

Objectives Continued

What do you think will happen in your relationship if you do nothing?

_____

_____

_____

_____

Rate your relationship in the first year of marriage (or if your not married, after you were together for a year)

With 1 being Unhappy and 5 being Ecstatic

1   2   3   4   5

Rate your relationship today

With 1 being Unhappy and 5 being Ecstatic

1   2   3   4   5

Come back to this page and rate your relationship after 1 month of working on your love languages.

With 1 being Unhappy and 5 being Ecstatic

1   2   3   4   5

... after 3 months of working on your love languages.

With 1 being Unhappy and 5 being Ecstatic

1   2   3   4   5

... after 6 months of working on your love languages.

With 1 being Unhappy and 5 being Ecstatic

1   2   3   4   5

... after 1 year of working on your love languages.

With 1 being Unhappy and 5 being Ecstatic

1   2   3   4   5

Brainstorm - Partner

Brainstorm a list of some of the things you could do for your partner in each of the 2 love languages.

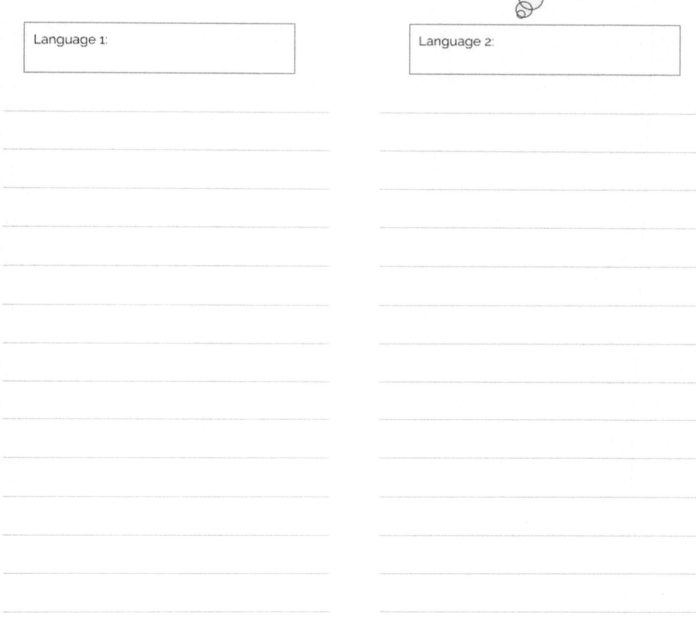

Language 1:

Language 2:

Brainstorm - You

Brainstorm a list of some of the things you would like your partner to do for you in each of the 2 love languages.

Language 1:	Language 2:

Month 1 – Your Partner

What do you want to experiment with this month? Take items from your brainstorm list and list them here. As you do them, check them off and also write the reaction you got from your partner. Have your partner complete a set as well..

	Action	Language	Reaction
☐			
☐			
☐			
☐			
☐			
☐			
☐			
☐			
☐			

How full is your partner's love tank?
(Scale of 1-10 with 10 being completely full) _____

Month 1 - You

Write down all the things your partner does for you this month and how each made you feel. Pay attention to his/her actions. Ask for what you want if you are not getting it.

Action	Reaction

How full is your love tank?
(Scale of 1-10 with 10 being completely full)   _____

Month 2 – Your Partner

Now that you have a month under your belt, look back and see what worked and what didn't. Try out a different dialect this month and adjust your approach to see if you can improve your results. Again, have your partner do the exercise as well.

	Action	Language	Reaction
☐			
☐			
☐			
☐			
☐			
☐			
☐			
☐			
☐			

How full is your partner's love tank?
(Scale of 1-10 with 10 being completely full) _____

Month 2 - You

Again, pay attention to what your partner does to fill your love tank. If your tank isn't getting filled, you need to get better at asking. It's ok to ask. Your partner is not a mind reader.

Action	Reaction

How full is your love tank?
(Scale of 1-10 with 10 being completely full) _____

Month 3 – Your Partner

You're two months in now. You should be getting a better idea of what your partner's true love language is and the dialect you need to use. Plan out your actions again this month.

	Action	Language	Reaction
☐			
☐			
☐			
☐			
☐			
☐			
☐			
☐			
☐			

How full is your partner's love tank?
(Scale of 1-10 with 10 being completely full) _____

Month 3 – You

By now you should have seen an improvement in your relationship. If not, again, ASK. Also, pay attention. Perhaps your partner is trying but his/her dialect is off target. Help him/her understand what you need.

Action	Reaction

How full is your love tank?
(Scale of 1-10 with 10 being completely full) _____

Results

Now that you have had three months of practice, go back to the rating page from earlier and rate your relationship at the 3-month mark. Has it improved? Have your partner rate the relationship as well.

Reflect as a couple by answering the questions below together.

How has your relationship changed over the past 3 months?

_____

_____

_____

_____

_____

Do you feel that you are moving closer to your ideal relationship and in what ways?

_____

_____

_____

_____

_____

Future Ideas – Your Partner

What will you do to make filling your partner's love tank a habit?

_____

_____

_____

_____

_____

_____

_____

_____

_____

_____

_____

_____

_____

_____

_____

_____

_____

_____

_____

_____

Future Ideas – You

What ideas do you have for your partner to make filling your love tank a habit for him/her?

_____

_____

_____

_____

_____

_____

_____

_____

_____

_____

_____

_____

_____

_____

_____

_____

Anniversary Journal

Track how you grow as a couple by journaling about your relationship each year.

Anniversary Journal

Year of:

_____
(Dates)

Our

_____
(Years)

Anniverary

Challenges

What were the biggest challenges you faced as a couple this past year and how did you handle them?

_____

_____

_____

_____

_____

_____

_____

_____

_____

_____

_____

_____

_____

_____

_____

_____

Greatest Moments

What were the highlights and greatest moments of this past year?

_____

_____

_____

_____

_____

_____

_____

_____

_____

_____

_____

_____

_____

_____

_____

_____

_____

Growth

How did you grow as a couple this past year?

_____

_____

_____

_____

_____

_____

_____

_____

_____

_____

_____

_____

_____

_____

_____

_____

Future

What are your hopes and goals for the future as a couple?

_____
_____
_____
_____
_____
_____
_____
_____
_____
_____
_____
_____
_____
_____
_____

Anniversary Journal

Year of:

_____
(Dates)

Our

_____
(Years)

Anniverary

Challenges

What were the biggest challenges you faced as a couple this past year and how did you handle them?

_____

_____

_____

_____

_____

_____

_____

_____

_____

_____

_____

_____

_____

_____

_____

_____

_____

_____

Greatest Moments

What were the highlights and greatest moments of this past year?

_____

_____

_____

_____

_____

_____

_____

_____

_____

_____

_____

_____

_____

_____

_____

Growth

How did you grow as a couple this past year?

_____
_____
_____
_____
_____
_____
_____
_____
_____
_____
_____
_____
_____
_____
_____
_____

Future

What are your hopes and goals for the future as a couple?

_____

_____

_____

_____

_____

_____

_____

_____

_____

_____

_____

_____

_____

_____

_____

_____

_____

_____

Anniversary Journal

Year of:

_____
(Dates)

Our

_____
(Years)

Anniverary

Challenges

What were the biggest challenges you faced as a couple this past year and how did you handle them?

_____

_____

_____

_____

_____

_____

_____

_____

_____

_____

_____

_____

_____

_____

_____

_____

Greatest Moments

What were the highlights and greatest moments of this past year?

_____

_____

_____

_____

_____

_____

_____

_____

_____

_____

_____

_____

_____

_____

_____

_____

Growth

How did you grow as a couple this past year?

_____

_____

_____

_____

_____

_____

_____

_____

_____

_____

_____

_____

_____

_____

_____

_____

Future

What are your hopes and goals for the future as a couple?

_____

_____

_____

_____

_____

_____

_____

_____

_____

_____

_____

_____

_____

_____

_____

_____

_____

_____

_____

Anniversary Journal

Year of:

_____
(Dates)

Our

_____
(Years)

Anniverary

Challenges

What were the biggest challenges you faced as a couple this past year and how did you handle them?

_____

_____

_____

_____

_____

_____

_____

_____

_____

_____

_____

_____

_____

_____

_____

_____

_____

_____

_____

Greatest Moments

What were the highlights and greatest moments of this past year?

_____

_____

_____

_____

_____

_____

_____

_____

_____

_____

_____

_____

_____

_____

_____

_____

Growth

How did you grow as a couple this past year?

_____

_____

_____

_____

_____

_____

_____

_____

_____

_____

_____

_____

_____

_____

_____

_____

_____

_____

_____

_____

Future

What are your hopes and goals for the future as a couple?

_____

_____

_____

_____

_____

_____

_____

_____

_____

_____

_____

_____

_____

_____

_____

_____

_____

Anniversary Journal

Year of:

_____
(Dates)

Our

_____
(Years)

Anniverary

Challenges

What were the biggest challenges you faced as a couple this past year and how did you handle them?

_____

_____

_____

_____

_____

_____

_____

_____

_____

_____

_____

_____

_____

_____

_____

_____

_____

_____

Greatest Moments

What were the highlights and greatest moments of this past year?

_____

_____

_____

_____

_____

_____

_____

_____

_____

_____

_____

_____

_____

_____

_____

_____

_____

_____

Growth

How did you grow as a couple this past year?

_____

_____

_____

_____

_____

_____

_____

_____

_____

_____

_____

_____

_____

_____

_____

_____

_____

_____

Future

What are your hopes and goals for the future as a couple?

_____

_____

_____

_____

_____

_____

_____

_____

_____

_____

_____

_____

_____

_____

_____

_____

_____

_____

Anniversary Journal

Year of:

_____
(Dates)

Our

_____
(Years)

Anniverary

Challenges

What were the biggest challenges you faced as a couple this past year and how did you handle them?

_____

_____

_____

_____

_____

_____

_____

_____

_____

_____

_____

_____

_____

_____

_____

_____

_____

_____

Greatest Moments

What were the highlights and greatest moments of this past year?

_____

_____

_____

_____

_____

_____

_____

_____

_____

_____

_____

_____

_____

_____

_____

Growth

How did you grow as a couple this past year?

_____

_____

_____

_____

_____

_____

_____

_____

_____

_____

_____

_____

_____

_____

_____

_____

_____

_____

Future

What are your hopes and goals for the future as a couple?

_____

_____

_____

_____

_____

_____

_____

_____

_____

_____

_____

_____

_____

_____

_____

_____

_____

_____

Anniversary Journal

Year of:

_____
(Dates)

Our

_____
(Years)

Anniverary

Challenges

What were the biggest challenges you faced as a couple this past year and how did you handle them?

_____

_____

_____

_____

_____

_____

_____

_____

_____

_____

_____

_____

_____

_____

_____

_____

Greatest Moments

What were the highlights and greatest moments of this past year?

_____

_____

_____

_____

_____

_____

_____

_____

_____

_____

_____

_____

_____

_____

_____

_____

Growth

How did you grow as a couple this past year?

_____

_____

_____

_____

_____

_____

_____

_____

_____

_____

_____

_____

_____

_____

_____

_____

_____

_____

_____

Future

What are your hopes and goals for the future as a couple?

_____

_____

_____

_____

_____

_____

_____

_____

_____

_____

_____

_____

_____

_____

_____

_____

_____

Anniversary Journal

Year of:

_____

(Dates)

Our

_____

(Years)

Anniverary

Challenges

What were the biggest challenges you faced as a couple this past year and how did you handle them?

_____

_____

_____

_____

_____

_____

_____

_____

_____

_____

_____

_____

_____

_____

_____

_____

_____

Greatest Moments

What were the highlights and greatest moments of this past year?

_____

_____

_____

_____

_____

_____

_____

_____

_____

_____

_____

_____

_____

_____

_____

_____

Growth

How did you grow as a couple this past year?

_____
_____
_____
_____
_____
_____
_____
_____
_____
_____
_____
_____
_____
_____
_____
_____

Future

What are your hopes and goals for the future as a couple?

_____

_____

_____

_____

_____

_____

_____

_____

_____

_____

_____

_____

_____

_____

_____

_____

_____

Anniversary Journal

Year of:

_____
(Dates)

Our

_____
(Years)

Anniverary

Challenges

What were the biggest challenges you faced as a couple this past year and how did you handle them?

_____

_____

_____

_____

_____

_____

_____

_____

_____

_____

_____

_____

_____

_____

_____

_____

_____

_____

Greatest Moments

What were the highlights and greatest moments of this past year?

_____

_____

_____

_____

_____

_____

_____

_____

_____

_____

_____

_____

_____

_____

_____

_____

_____

Growth

How did you grow as a couple this past year?

_____

_____

_____

_____

_____

_____

_____

_____

_____

_____

_____

_____

_____

_____

_____

_____

_____

_____

Future

What are your hopes and goals for the future as a couple?

_____

_____

_____

_____

_____

_____

_____

_____

_____

_____

_____

_____

_____

_____

_____

_____

_____

Anniversary Journal

Year of:

_____
(Dates)

Our

_____
(Years)

Anniverary

Challenges

What were the biggest challenges you faced as a couple this past year and how did you handle them?

_____

_____

_____

_____

_____

_____

_____

_____

_____

_____

_____

_____

_____

_____

_____

_____

_____

_____

Greatest Moments

What were the highlights and greatest moments of this past year?

Growth

How did you grow as a couple this past year?

_____
_____
_____
_____
_____
_____
_____
_____
_____
_____
_____
_____
_____
_____
_____
_____
_____

Future

What are your hopes and goals for the future as a couple?

_____

_____

_____

_____

_____

_____

_____

_____

_____

_____

_____

_____

_____

_____

_____

_____

76468047R00043

Made in the USA
Columbia, SC
24 September 2019